Tragedies of Love

by

Michelle Rene Scott

DORRANCE PUBLISHING CO
EST. 1920
PITTSBURGH, PENNSYLVANIA 15238

Dorrance Publishing Co
585 Alpha Drive
Suite 103
Pittsburgh, PA 15238
Visit our website at *www.dorrancebookstore.com*

ISBN: 979-8-8860-4336-5
eISBN: 979-8-8860-4501-7

Table of Contents

Acknowledgments

"Crazy" was previously featured in "Essence of a Dream" – The National Library of Poetry, "James Bonamy" was a poem I wrote about James Bonamy & his wife. I wrote the poem for a radio contest to win tickets to his upcoming show and a meet and greet. I wrote it, called the station, read it on air, and won my tickets and my meet and greet.

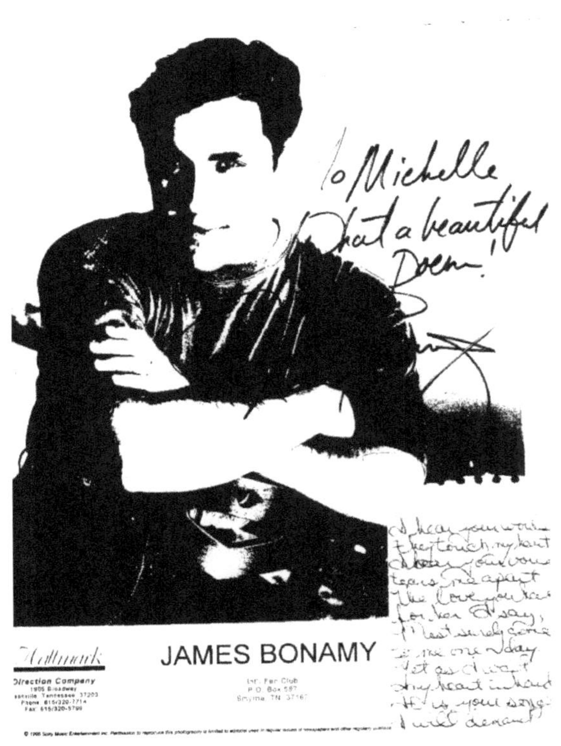

Reality, Truth, & Trust

The truth so hard to see it, as it stares you in the face,

there's shame that swells within you, yet it's handled

with such grace.

The world I see around me, created only in my mind,

makes me struggle with reality, for me not easy to define.

I've drawn a line between them, reality and truth,

my mind succumbed to fantasy, for me I must have proof.

Proving truth can drive you crazy, as it is plain to see,

if you need a live example, just take a look at me.

Now let's throw in another twist, the issue known as trust,

please know trust is not a given, to prove it is a must.

If truth can drive you crazy, trust will shoot you to the moon

and if you're not aware of this, you will be very soon.

Life takes you down so many roads, and some are not so nice

but those roads become a part of you, it's just the way of life.

For me, my roads are guilty of driving me insane

but doctors say that's not the case, crossed circuits are to blame.

I know that they are doctors, with white coats and PhD's

and certainly deserve respect, that's what they'll get from me.

But what they must remember, is that I live in this brain,

so, who's to say who's better at diagnosing me insane?

My world, as you see it, is a complicated place,

so, I've had to set up boundaries as I'm running out of space.

So please don't take it personally if I don't let you in,

it's just the over-crowding is making my head spin.

And I am truly sorry that you are missing out

cause there's never a dull moment when Shelly is about.

Me and Me2

Why should you want to remember good days of love now gone?

You do it on your own time you can't make me your pawn.

We were doing fine why would you bring up all this shit?

Don't you dare show any weakness or you know I'll throw a fit!

Must I remind you of all the scars left on our heart?

The scars that made us who we are so we will never part.

Should we ever part with our scars we lose who we really are.

So, zip your lip, never speak of love as it just becomes a scar.

Scars

What else will you take from me? Was eight years not enough?

Why is it that you shadow me? You make living life so tough.

Are you happy that you've done it? You might say you think you've won.

Cause the scars you left upon me are too deep to overcome.

They take the love I have for him and twist it all around.

Until that one last little twist, then no longer is love found.

How could it be the scars you left could have so much control?

I think I know the answer, they consume my heart and soul.

I know they'll never be another love for me as I loved you.

But I must continue living knowing other loves won't be as true.

I'm asking for the slightest break, ease off the scars that bind me.

You cannot control the scars you left they're mine to put behind me.

Now that's a sucky situation, I own the scars you left that will

not heal.

Seems this molehill is a mountain I did not bargain for this deal.

I ponder on the question of what to do with scars so deep?

I'd take a knife and cut them out, from you so I must keep.

Cause if I did not keep them then I'd lose memories of our love.

And I could never let that happen, you were the dream I'd always

dreamed of.

Okay, that's it, I'm ready. I'll live my life the best I can.

And yes I'll let the scars come too since they are who I am.

Razor's Edge

When I close my eyes and think of you, cuts me swift like razors edge.

With an edge so fine like a thinly drawn line hides the measure of its depth.

So, who's to know if it cut to my soul, eyes upon me as I wept?

When I close my eyes and think of you, cuts me wounded, cuts me dead?

First, remember the time when you were once mine held on like you'd never let go.

Yet I could feel the blade slide over my skin with your touch I had no way to know.

I can feel your large hands slide over me soon the fire within me glows.

Although danger lies around each curve there's no stopping as passion grows.

I need your hands to smooth over me as the blade glides over
my skin.
How could I have known they were one in the same,
the nightmare was soon to begin.

Now that you're done with me, the passion once felt for me
starts to fade.
You wait like a snake to be free of me, straight through my heart
with your blade.

My Turn Pretender

I know now I cannot go to where I have just been.

He took me, he cut me, then he drove the knife in.

Never once made a promise as to how this might end.

So he smiles with false innocence as he calls me "his friend."

The pretender of honesty and truth he did lure me.

Gave me hope for a love that he knew well wouldn't be.

Yet day after day he still took my love,

took my heart, took my soul, took my dreams I dreamed of.

The touches we gave, the love that we made,

Now just a memory beginning to fade.

But the scars from the knife they don't fade, they don't heal.

Just reminds me of pretender and my love he did steal.

So now I am finished, never going to this place I've just been.

For I've had it with pretenders and the pain they cause within.

So pretender of emotions should we ever meet again.

Don't be surprised to see I've changed new endeavors I begin.

Can't you guess how I've changed? What is it don't you see?

I'm coming back strong as pretender, look in the mirror. "It is

me!"

My Mind is a Cyclone

My mind is like a cyclone, thoughts spinning in my head.

The pieces of debris try to escape the fear of dread.

I try so hard to make them ascend into the sky.

Yet the power of this cyclone pulls them back within to fly.

There's nothing I can do I just have to let them spin.

Hoping soon that they will weaken slowly letting peace within.

I know it's only temporary for the cyclone never dies.

Tricks me into feeling peace as the wind picks up and flies.

Crazy

____

So you say I'm crazy loving you the way I do,

my jealous fits of anger keep on breaking through.

The nights they pass and with the dawn,

we ask each other, "What went wrong?"

The question isn't easy and seldom answers come

but deep inside where the craziness lies, blames set on only one.

See you can't make me crazy, nor can you break my heart,

crazy only came but once, I "lost it" fell apart.

And broken hearts they say will mend, how fortunate, so true,

it's then the mind protects the heart, with bitterness all through.

So yes, I may be crazy as bitter words fly from bitter tongue

but you see, they're just protection from a love that has begun.

Still, I could say, "I love you," and I'd mean every word

but what was said in silence is what you should have heard.

A heart breaks once and then it mends

so sad the bitter on it depends.

Oh, bitterness you shield my heart,

you shield my love, is there no new start?

So yes, I say I'm crazy loving you the way I do

but crazy wouldn't be all bad if you were crazy loving me too.

Strong Enough

Am I strong enough to take this? Am I strong enough to stay?

Am I strong enough to feel your touch, then watch you

walk away?

Will my feelings not grow deeper every time we kiss?

Will my heart not break tomorrow giving in to love like this?

Why can't I just accept you just the way you are?

Why must I keep on dreaming wishing on a fallen star?

What don't I understand about the words you speak so clear?

What don't you understand about my actions when I near?

Don't we both see the paths we take are not one in the same?

Don't we both see that neither is the only one to blame?

With our wants and needs so different are we truly being fair?

With us knowing that the love I seek from you just isn't there.

So once again I ask myself am I able to be strong?

Can I bear the pain and sorrow of holding on to love that's

wrong?

I'm not quite sure just what I'll do about this love I'm in.

I'm not quite sure, should I hear your words that I'll not hurt

again.

So am I strong enough to take this? Am I strong enough to stay?

Am I strong enough to give you up and now just walk away?

I know I must in time give up this love I feel for you,

but now, no I'm not strong enough to tell my heart we're

through.

How Can I Help You?

How can I help you let go of a love?

A touch of my hand, a tender kiss from my lips?

It will take so much more to let go love such as this.

How can I help you let go of a love?

Give a shoulder to cry on, just someone to hold?

Could this be enough to let go love grown old?

How can I help you let go of a love?

Make your nights no so lonely, give my love so free?

How often I've wondered, are your thoughts then of me?

How can I help you let go of a love?

Willingly offer my heart, mind & soul?

Or has your heart grown so weary it's taken its toll?

How can I help you let go of a love?

Be patient and wait, give your heart time to heal?

Not something I'm good at, but for you, wait, I will.

For you see Father Time remains my good friend.

He whispers to me nightly, "see this through to the end."

So, my love please forgive me, but I'm asking once more,

Can't you see that I must cause it's you I adore?

So, tell me, please tell me…

How can I help you let go of a love?

The choice remains yours, choose any, choose all.

Just please make a choice so I don't take a fall.

How can I help you let go of a love?

Your choice I'll make easy, giving all mentioned above.

Little Feelings

Every time I see you, each time I hear your voice

I get that "little feeling," it comes without a choice.

Not to say I'd choose repression and hide this feeling deep

within

it's just a little frightening if you knew just where I'd been.

Not to say I've not been warned, oh yes, they echo in my ear,

and not to say I didn't listen, but it's him I want to hear.

I long to get to know you, see the you, you really are

your voice, your touch, your laughter, superb is what you've

shown so far.

But then I get that "little feeling" that just won't go away

"Little feeling" deep inside me – you cannot come out to play!

Cause I know just where I want to be, with life I am content,

but now I've got that "little feeling", and I'm not sure what I

meant.

Cause I know this "little feeling" and it does not come alone
it's brought along its baggage packed with questions I won't
own.

So, repress my "little feelings"? Absolutely I will not.
Just its questions I will filter, no grounds to hit this pot!

I may have slipped already, but I don't think I did,
I just asked the burning question it came straight from my head.

"Little feelings" did not play a part…okay, a minor role,
but twas logic pushed it from my tongue and logic has control.

It was not my "little feelings" asking, "Do you have another?"
It was the consequences that I faced had you answered other.

Now the question I have asked and the answer I have heard
and my logic has accepted, "Little feelings" – Not a word!

You see I got the answer, the one I so needed to hear.
Time to zip and lock the baggage "little feelings" hold so dear.

Logic unpacked the one that counts, that's all that matters now,
and with it you did get a glimpse of "little feelings" in Michelle.

My Love No More

I woke one day to find my love didn't love me anymore.

He went out one night without me, found himself at

another's door.

Is that all it took for you my love to leave me far behind?

One night in another's arms or had this been designed?

And now my love I love you not, for shallow you must be.

For no one but a shallow man could leave as you left me.

I know now you did not love me but for two years lived a lie.

And for this my love I hate you, I don't even have to try.

I should have seen betrayal hidden deep within your eyes.

I should have heard the words you spoke, knowing they were

lies.

I have little left to say my love for you exist to me no more.

You can take your lies with your demon eyes to that other

bitch's door.

I never will look back my love seeking memories of you.

I never could look back my love for those memories were not

you.

The Call

In just a few moments I'm going to call.

Last words with the devil I'm through with them all.

He will hear my words sharp, he will hear my words plain

Cast out all of his demons, let nothing remain.

Take now your possessions, your treachery, your lies

Let nothing remain here, not even goodbyes.

Fear Drove Love Away from Me

It would have made me crazy, had he decided to stay.

Old scars became new wounds, it was me drove him away.

I tried my best to tell him, let him know right from the start

that my past had done some damage, please be careful with

my heart.

I needed not just love, but true love I'd always yearned to know.

A love between two people, that does nothing else but grow.

With him I truly found the love I'd longed for all my years.

I can't believe such petty things sparked fire to hidden fears.

Little lies should be forgiven and would have been for most,

but he'd promised he would never lie and thus stirred up old

ghosts.

God knows I tried to let it go like a feather in the wind,

but I love him like no other and the fears came rushing in.

Fear then morphed into obsession, I had to know his love

I watched his every movement like a hawk that flies above.

Demands I made to quantify this love he felt for me.

Shrieked words of ultimatums, blind with fear I couldn't see.

I did not get the answers that would have calmed my fears.

Expectations when they're set too high can only bring forth

tears.

So, if he did once love me, as true a love as love could be

I lost the love I'd longed for as my fears drove him from me.

Fool

Fool to take the chance again.

Fool to think your heart could win.

True love is not your destiny,

sure pain is where your heart will be.

This man you see and hold so dear,

fool you fool, do you see him here?

Fool you fool, he loves you not.

Love is one-sided, or had you forgot?

Fool to think love would come your way.

You can love all you want – he won't feel the same way.

Lost Control

This is how I do it once I've lost control.

Putting pen to paper where I can bare my soul.

Tried to get you near me, kind of lost my head.

Words didn't come together so much more I should have said.

The last time that I saw you, not so long ago,

was my last chance I could have you, that's why I've lost control.

Because it didn't come together like I'd planned you see,

I should have been more forceful, then you would have come to

me.

Instead you made me crazy and the words just wouldn't come,

I melted in the moment and my chance was all but done.

And now I'll never see you, how the thought just chills my soul.

It kills me to admit it, now because of you I've lost control.

Go Ahead

Go ahead…

Make me go away.

Say the things you're wanting to say. Go Ahead.

Go ahead…

Feel for you and not for me

It's what you want, to just be free. Go ahead

Go ahead…

Take your chances 'free' out there

Despair, mistrust thick in the air. Go ahead

Go ahead…

Live your life as a shallow man

Get your kicks from your one-night stands. Go ahead

Go ahead…

Turn your back on this love

Not something a 'free man' should be thinking of. Go ahead

Go ahead…

Time to carry out your plan

This life you chose as a 'simple free man.' Go ahead

Don'Cha Know

Don'cha know how I know that you have another?

Don'cha know a woman knows when her man strains to cover?

Don'cha know your words change just as much as your actions?

Don'cha see you're getting upset over the tiniest infractions.

Don'cha know a woman sees straight to a man's soul?

Don'cha know ya can't cover it, push it, or pull?

Your woman's gonna see it, feel it, hear it, there's no doubt
about that.

Don'cha know it's not like keep'n a secret tucked beneath
that ballcap?

Hate to say it, "Yep I'm old but older in wisdom than in years."

I almost wish I wasn't, so I wouldn't worry or have fears.

Don'cha know how much I truly loved you in years past?

And I still would'da and I still could'da had you not fell for that trash

If you see me crying, just quickly walk on by,

cause once you get me crying, I'm sure to punch you in the eye.

Don't look surprised you shit for brains cause you're the one who

did it,

you took my love you chewed it up and then you went and spit

it.

Two Words

"I'm sorry" – these two words, important as the seem

I must show you through my actions or I will lose my dream.

"Forgive me" – these two words, important as they seem

must truly be accepted or <u>we</u> will lose <u>our</u> dream.

To share a life together will bring times the road gets rough

but we can overcome those times, our love is strong enough.

Giving In?

____

I came so close this time – reached out, could almost touch it.

Suppress the fears, forget the tears, how am I going to do it?

I closed my eyes and took a breath the feeling came again.

The feeling I had locked inside like Spring reborn within.

How my mind did race with thoughts of love – had the dreams I

dreamed come true?

Could this truly be the love I've longed for? This love I found in you?

The moment that I saw your eyes I knew you were the one.

The moment that you kissed my lips the feelings had begun.

This time I will not shield my heart it's you that I'll let in.

My bitterness I'll cast aside never to scar this heart again.

No more thoughts of chance or risk, these things don't

matter anymore.

I now release my feelings of love to run rampant like never before.

Behind Closed Doors

No one knows the darkness that lies behind closed doors.

It's when the darkness manifests into nightmares,

Your screams just echo off the walls.

Nobody hears them.

The doors remain closed.

Fear – No Words

I'm not quite sure what's going on, I've faced these fears before,

I've placed my shield of bitterness in front of my heart's door.

Yet my feel for you is different, bitter shield will be no more.

I take my chances or face the fact love stays on distant shores.

I'm never at a loss for words, especially with the pen,

But ever since you kissed my lips, fears crept up from deep

within.

What have I done by holding you, you've filled my mind com-

pletely?

So where are my words, as my thoughts of you should flow from

pen so sweetly.

The Storm | Part 1

With each storm new fears are born, turn back! No strength
to weather.
Yet a different storm not seen before hiding fears – I'm
not together.

Storms will not ask if I am ready nor do they care if you prepare,
Storms strike upon me swiftly reaping havoc and despair.

Yet there's something different with this storm as gentle
breezes blow.
No it's not the calm before the storm, that feeling I would know.

I cannot bear these feelings, as this storm will just not mark me.
So survive I will, yet hopeless still, cease ventures, alone I'll
make me.

The Storm | Part 2

I let myself get out here, where I don't belong.

The lightning flashes as thunder crashes brainstorm

much too strong.

Could weather it alone you see,

then distant storm is all would be.

Clear thoughts from days I thought were near,

I slowly think them, they disappear.

Past storms they tend to haunt me, knew better giving rise

to this storm.

Why wasn't I able to stop me, where was it I made

the wrong turn?

I tell myself I'm not afraid this storm won't overtake me.

Yet knowing well my fears are true it is this storm will break me.

False Truths

How hard it is to face false truths, when weaved precise to fit me.

Why will storms rise behind these eyes, if not just here to trick me?

Innocent Child

____

Innocent child, fearful young child, why did you hold your tears in?

Would they not made aware those you longed for to care the pain harbored so deep within?

I don't think they saw nor had even a clue as to what was made obvious to you.

So you built up your wall so fearful you'd fall built an image that was so untrue.

And now that you're grown, how could you have known they'd be rivals, this image and you.

Yet it can't go away, with you it must stay – there is purpose so must not undo.

Napkin Thought

Years fly by, yet time stands still for the heart

that cannot let go of a love that is timeless.

I hear your words they touch my heart.

I hear your voice tears me apart.

The love you have for her I say,

Must surely come to me one day.

Yet as I wait, my heart in hand

It is your songs I will demand.

Crumble & Fall

You dumb bitch, what happened to your wall?

You watched it crumble and yes you watched it fall.

Built solely for self-preservation a fortress to guard your heart.

Took years to master your techniques now you watch it fall apart?

Techniques you found through bitterness so strong could never

fail

Your weakness lets it crumble and fall now you've sent your mind

to hell.

Unprotected

I feel so unprotected now that my wall came crashing down.

I contemplate reconstruction, fear the man that did destroy it

may never come around.

I really have no worries of any unwanted approaches.

My years have made me crafted skills at crushing roaches.

The Wait

I told you I would wait, there's nothing else to do.

It's just a little different now since the wait is without you.

And I'm alright and it's okay, my memories will get me by.

And if and when you come back to me, I'll never question why

Why you left and why I cried will make no difference then,

Cause you'll be where you were meant to be, back in my

arms again.

Battles

Thought all the fights were over, all battles I had won.

Reality, it told me there was a battle left, last one.

This battle it was different, it was one I could not see.

The demon of the mind that lurked inside of me.

With God's help I saw victory as I neared the battles erd.

Not knowing this faceless battle would come back around

the bend.

Attempt

I thought that it was over

I thought that I was done.

I looked up to the bluest sky

Body soul warmed by the sun.

I found my inner strength to pull the reins in on my heart,

But just as I could feel control, thoughts of him ripped through

my heart.

I am not upset for losing the control I thought I had

First attempts at anything often fail but that's not bad.

Apparently my failed attempt to clear him from my mind

Proves I'm not quite ready to leave these feelings far behind.

Me2 to Me and My Pen

Wow, hello old friend long time no see.

I had to take a break to take a look at me.

We cannot say we missed you for she had no desire.

You know for her to touch you she has to be inspired.

We can tell that you're excited because you know just what

this means

We broke though the chains, the bars, the scares, yes, she's in

love it seems.

Now I can feel you hesitate, this was not part of our plan,

Yet I'm right here to stand by you to write til we understand.

So many things have happened to get us to this place

Of putting pen to paper another poem we'll embrace.

So sad times have been compiling our tragedies of life,

So glad to know that this one will reveal our love of life.

Yes, my friend, it's a Godsend we fell in love again,

Our heart no longer harbors past bitterness within.

The love we felt so strongly so many years ago

Has not ever left us, steadfast along our road.

Matters not the love we feel for him may not reciprocate

The home we had at Linda's brought forth courage to compete.

Our course gave us the strength to tell him how we feel.

To stop and think how brave we were, seems just so surreal.

What is so incredible is how we dealt with his response.

Wasn't quite what we were looking for yet try again we must.

Ponder

If I could have you ponder just a little longer just a little more,

eventually your pondering would lead you to my door.

I believe I'd give almost anything to see your face again,

Cause when our eyes met for the first time, I felt that feeling

deep within.

A feeling that I thought I had hidden far away,

How was it you were able to pull it from me in just one day?

I do wish you would ponder about me night and day.

That would justify my thoughts of you I can't get to go away.

As you ponder day and night, I won't ponder you at all.

For you see that is impossible, cause I've built up a wall.

No, no, no, fact is there will be no pondering here

Fact is I want this fact to be made perfectly clear.

So sad I cannot ponder, as you ponder day and night

Fact is I'm full of bullshit cause I ponder you all right.

Love at First Sight

I have a question for you, do you believe in love at first sight?

I never thought I did until I met a man one steamy night.

One night? I say, "wait!," just a physical attraction

but I knew better as it was my soul controlled my reaction.

As we sat talking, I felt he could see straight through me.

As if he read my mind as these feelings shot through me.

I found love at first sight is a true living feeling

but it's not worth a damn if a ring he is wearing.

And so that's how it ended, my love at first sight,

He belonged to another and there was my plight.

It never happened before, hope it won't happen again

As love at first sight holds such mysteries within.

Dreams

As I lay me down to sleep, I close my eyes to see

The man who's turned my life around, the man who's set me free.

Free from all the bitterness I'd built up throughout my years,

Didn't think I'd ever feel again, my heart knew only tears.

Now as I lay here, thoughts of you, I know will never fade

for as slumber over comes me you're from what my dreams are

made.

Though tonight I cannot touch you, I'll touch you in my dreams.

We'll hold each other through the night, how right to me

this seems.

When daybreak brings in rays of sun that falls upon my face.

I'll wake to be alone again, it's my dreams I must embrace.

A Spy

If ever a time I controlled my own thoughts,

To think of you again, I certainly would not.

Does it give you a kick seeing me fall apart?

I'm not falling apart, it's just a feel in my heart.

Of course not, you don't see me unless you're a spy,

Cause I never see you, and I never lie.

In one respect yes, I wish you a spy,

Cause then I would know I still catch your eye.

Dream that sweet dream that he cared as to spy,

Cause you know it's all bullshit, and I never lie.

Release

I release you from me, you may now go away.

It's not that I ever even asked you to stay.

But you bullied my brain into thinking of you,

Now I'm bullying back, thoughts of you they are through!

Yeah right, took the words right out of my mouth,

Cause we neither are bullies, so I'll go to "time out."

Out of My Dreams Out of My Head

I'm done writing about you, get out of my head!

Now I'm turning the lights out and I'm going to bed!

And oh, by the way, please stay out of my dreams.

As I just cannot take this, can you not hear my screams?

Okay, this is it, my pen I put down.

Now listen to me, I'm not fooling around.

You stay out of my dreams; you stay out of my head.

 This is the last time I'm telling you, "I'm going to bed!"

For all of my life I've controlled my own dreams

Unfortunately, my thoughts kind of do their own thing.

With that being said, a compromise will be needed

Cause once put to the pen the words have been seeded.

Since my thoughts are gonna do what my thoughts are gonna do,

I'll reluctantly allow my thoughts to continue thinking of you.

Once daylight turns to darkness and my body needs to sleep,

I'll close my eyes to dream my dreams, from you don't want a peep.

Okay I guess the deal is done there's nothing more need be said.
Except one thing I have to say, "I'm now going to bed!"

Teardrop

My dear what is that I see?

A teardrop down your cheek could be?

Is it the storm that makes you cry?

Or maybe they're just raindrops falling from the sky.

I touch your cheek where droplet lies.

Put to my tongue can't be disguised.

I taste the salt hence where it came.

It is a tear, can't be the rain.

I know not where this tear hath come.

Your past has past you've overcome.

My dear, your past is present, I fear.

How close is he, is he far or near?

Your silence tells me many things.

You won't give up what secrets bring.

I know you so much more than others,

Frightens me for you, that I can't uncover.

Another tear runs down your face,

It must be love that you've embraced.

Your silence cannot fool me,

You're in love it's plain to see.

As I watch your face & wait for words from within

There's something wrong with this love that you're in.

You sit silent in the rain and cry

You silence your secret – I wonder why?

Just know that I am here for you, just as our Lord above.

And He's the one no silence comes He knows your secret love.

Now dry your tears and end your fears,

God is with you through all your years.

Dreams Lost

The pain may ease as days go by, the world still turning round

but the dream I'd hoped to share with you no longer can be

found.

To share a dream with someone, the two become as "one"

To lose one or the other, the "one" slips into none.

The dream then dies forever, fading memories in the mind

for no one's left to find them, forever lost in time.

Lone Tree

A tree stands alone in a clearing.

Looking out at the horizon seeing the forest oh so clear.

Then realizes the distance that will never bring them near.

The lone tree's not unhappy she can dream of being with them

She's healthy and stands tall watching her distant forest friends.

So far from one another yet so much they have in common

For her beauty changes just as they, with every passing season.

That One October Night

The fire crackled in the stove the room was toasty warm.

The candles flicker as shadows danced no power with this

ice storm.

Yet as I set by fire's glow, I felt something was not right.

Thoughts of leaving my snug home burned within me that one

October night.

I felt a chill go up my spine as I sat wrapped in my blanket

What drew me to the glass doors to gaze out at the darkness?

I felt weary as my knees gave way thoughts rushing through

my mind.

The hauntings of past lost loves, thoughts believed left far be-

hind.

I have no recollection of how the door did open nor how I

got outside,

I know my feet never touched the ground it was like a ghost I glide.

Yet suddenly there I was standing still amongst the trees.

Ice so heavy on their limbs unable to move with the breeze.

It seemed so strange the bitter cold did not sting my senses.

Then once again old memories came rushing in breaking down

all my defenses.

What caused these thoughts to overcome my mind to leave bu-

ried took all my might.

But come they did and would not leave that one October night.

Then once again my knees gave way my eyes did flutter closed.

I felt chilled arms wrap around me and with these arms I rose.

Rose not just to my feet you see, these arms weren't of this earth.

I fought so hard to free myself, yet my struggles had no worth.

With my strength almost depleted I fought with all my might.

I guess they had somewhere to take me that one October night.

And then I woke to find myself locked up in my own mind.

Chilled arms no longer bound me yet locked up no key to find.

I was forced to watch each memory of lost loves just pass me by
I wanted to break free from them, I wanted them to die.

I fought hard, yet unable to make them go away
Trapped in my mind with painful thoughts I'd stay.

I do not dare peak out to see who might be peaking in.
Cause if it's one that put me here his life is sure to end.

Now I'm still here just watching as each memory brings forth pain.
At times I see someone watching me and they know I am insane.

I pay no attention to those outside my mind, for I know that they are right.
Insane I am, insane I'll stay since old ghosts did overtake me that one October night.

____

Dear Lord,

Help me to find the faith in You to know that the decisions that I make for my life are guided by You. That You are forever with me, whether in times of loneliness and sorrow or happiness and joy. That You have a reason for all that happens. That my doubts shall be softened by my faith and my love for You. That Thy will be done. Through Jesus Christ,

Amen

My Sleep Prayer

Dear Father God,

Night is here – soon sleep will overcome me. Oh, how I used to love my sleep.

Please bring back my love of sleep. So, I'll say my prayers and let You choose which ones to answer.

For I know He has a plan for me so sleep and dreams for me are now His alone.

Through Jesus Christ,

Amen

My Children

I guess my days are numbered, I'm just like all the rest

I think about the life I've lived and pray I did my best.

The best for my two children whom I love with all my heart

and pray they have forgiven me for when I made them part.

The question that still haunts me, "Did I do right by them?"

I made a tough decision, tore my soul so deep within.

To think I was the cause for any suffering or pain,

creates an ache within me, no words could possibly explain.

Sometimes I stop and wonder, did I harm their love for me?

God, I pray that's not the case, their love is life to me.

Day In the Sun with God

As the sun beats down upon my face

I know I wouldn't be here had it not been for Your grace.

Sweat beads upon my forehead as the skies are drenched with

sun

In the distance I hear giggles as the children splash in fun.

I know that You watch over them just as parents do

I pray someday they find the grace that's only found in You.

The heat now penetrates my skin travels deeply to my bones

I'll stay here waiting patiently until You call me home.

Til then I'll watch Your miracle of how my flowers grow.

My home blessed with Your beauty gives sweet fragrance

for the soul.

For all cried tears throughout the years would never trade a one.

For those tears watered my spirit, now feels life has just begun.

Heartaches

God can lift the hurt you're feeling, He can take away each care
But you must give Him all your burdens and that's only done
through prayer.

God knows everything about you from the beginning to the end.
He can help you like no other, He's your very dearest friend.

When you are weak, He'll make you strong, when you are sad He
brings such peace
When you're discouraged, He's right with you, then you will feel
God's sweet release.

He'll walk with you through each valley, till the mountain you as-
cend
And it's only through His comfort that a broken heart can mend.

Don't allow your faith to falter, don't give up, keep pressing on.
You can make it with the Lord's help, after darkness comes
the dawn.

God's Plan

My racing thoughts have slowed now, doesn't mean they've
gone away.
But just the mention of our Father God keeps the racing
thoughts at bay.

Will I stay here in my safe place confined day after day?
It is through prayer Father God will always show the way.

The bitch inside is gone now, thank you Jesus for your grace.
The Lord against my racing thoughts will always win the race.

The comfort that He brings me can only come from Him.
God help me through these troubled times & keep my life from
sin.

Only You can understand me and ease my troubled mind.
Why is it I keep seeking for the man I'll never find?

I ache for love of flesh and blood, a partner for my life.
I thought I'd found him recently then found he had a wife.

I dare not hold within me any feelings I felt for him.

As feelings for a married man must surely be a sin.

And so, this ache for love I hold I give unto God's hands.

I'll be content with life whatever You have planned.

What Lies Ahead

As time draws nearer in my life, another page to turn.

Not sure of how I am to feel, feel nothing I discern.

Uncertain of what lies ahead, I dare not even ponder.

Life holds so many mysteries, allows the mind to wonder.

Not to guess what lies ahead with the pages yet to turn,

Would like a peek into tomorrow to see if I get burned.

I fear a life of loneliness will be my final page.

Was unaware life's sorrows would follow me with age.

I won't have time to reconcile with each event that haunts me.

To live my final days in peace outweighs the ache inside me.

I won't allow my days gone by to harbor in my soul.

The joy of life and love I have is what will make me whole.

Dark Skies

Dark skies, rain is near

Thunder crashes, lightning flashes

Reminder to us God is near.

Wind blows as trees sway

Breaking pieces blown away.

God brings me peace when I'm afraid

He's by my side, He's never strayed.

The storms that I'm afraid of are blessings from above

The raindrops pouring from the skies are just droplets of His

love.

Thunder speaks His power

Lightning shows His might

The greatness of God's glory

Is never far from sight.

Life Intended

She sits all alone on her front porch swing, in a house far too big

for one person to live.

Yes, she lives all alone in that great big home, because she gave

all herself she could give.

She remembers a day when love came her way,

yet she also remembers love never could stay.

So vivid the memories with the distance of centuries, not one

love was she able to save.

As tears swell in her eyes the heartache still thrives, and the scars

she will take to her grave.

She knows God never intended to leave her unmended,

feels comfort by His Will being transcended.

She has so many years filled with unnumbered blessings; she

feels shameful to hang on to past sorrows.

With her hands slightly shaking helped along with some blinking,

dries her tears, it's His Will that she follows.

She lived out her days on her front porch swing, in a house far

too big for one person to live.

Yes, she lived all alone in that great big home, now happy she

gave all she could give.

The Lord took her Home and was there she was shown how her

life had affected so many.

God's Will had been done, and as her words through her son

began their destined journey.

Ease My Troubled Mind

If I could fly, I'd fly away, soaring through the deepest blue

Not caring where I'm going, mind clear of thoughts of you.

I'd look above – The Heavens, I'd look below – the ground

Not knowing where I'm going, just in hopes I'll not be found.

The breeze it blows my hair back, crisp air it stings my face

I'm climbing through the clouds now, soon memories erased.

So close, I know He's out there, so further I must climb.

For He's the one can save me, can erase my troubled mind.

I know that He has watched me slip from time to time,

Yet I know that He'll embrace me and ease my troubled mind.

He gave me life to live and learn, I did as best I could,

And now I'm going home to Him to live the life I should.

There has never been One greater, or never One so kind.

Now My Lord with you forever, you've eased my troubled mind.

Tragedies of Love

I must have seen it coming, why did I shut my eyes?

Closed they would have been remaining, had it not been for

your lies.

And the words I wrote so bittersweet as if my hand did know,

they would be a sad reminder of where this heart would go.

Now my nights are full of sadness as the loneliness sinks in,

even slumber that once brought me peace, brings pain from

deep within.

Now my eyes are surely open, yet I see through blur and haze

like my life is now another's, different time with different days.

My life's now changed forever, with my hopes and dreams to

dust.

Learn to live with pain and sorrow, I tell myself I must.

My thoughts of you I count on to surely fade with time,

yet I know the scars left on my heart forever will be mine.

Mine to try and cover, mine to try and hide.

My scars a sad reminder of a love should never died.

How long it takes for my eyes to clear and my broken heart to

mend,

does not really matter for the scars stay till my end.

Then once my eyes have closed for good, my last breath I have

taken,

I suddenly see clear, no haze, as if I'd been awakened.

And all the pain and sorrow I tried to deal with all my days,

were unable to come with me and for this I give You praise.

And the scars that once bore burden to my heart with no relief,

like my pain and sorrow no longer with me, no longer cause

me grief.

This truly must be Heaven, with no pain, no scars, no sorrow.

And You've promised me these days will last, here today is

here tomorrow.

There's one last thing I'll leave behind My Lord won't take above,

It is the words this hand once wrote, my "Tragedies of Love"